IF YOU'RE LUCKY
IS A THEORY
OF MINE

IF YOU'RE LUCKY
IS A THEORY OF MINE

NORMAL

I FEEL SORRY FOR YOU

What will you do when you wake up one morning
to find that god's made you plain?

—Billy Bragg

Prologue

In the 1950s, so-called "normal" people were solicited to take part in LSD experiments at the VA Hospital in Los Angeles. Researchers wanted to learn how lysergic acid, once consumed, affected these people. One subject, deemed a normal housewife, drank, while being filmed, a small amount of LSD in a glass of water. During her trip, the researcher, Dr. Sidney Cohen, interviewed her. "If you can't see it then you'll just never know" is the conclusion the subject came to after several failed attempts to explain to Dr. Cohen what she was seeing. Just prior to saying, "If you can't see it then you'll just never know," the subject said, "I wish I could talk in Technicolor." Just after, when the implications of not being able to translate what she saw and felt for the researcher became clear, the subject said, "I feel sorry for you."

IF YOU CAN'T SEE IT THEN
YOU'LL JUST NEVER KNOW

To survive is to lament, so let's all do it well

Say some coffee spills in a lap, a Toyota loses control,
crosses my path and takes me out. How long until

you, half drunk drinking from your happily-ever-after straw,
in your not-me, not-today chair in the sun,

hear the news?

The closest you'll get to ghost life in this life,
to hovering like the warm-breathed peacock of elegiac praise

over your own funeral,

is horizon to horizon satellite coverage of the city in which you live
when a bridge of magnitude, which stood for fifty years in opposition

to the custom of not saying hello to the strangers you pass in the city,
taps out.

I say this standing behind the beloved dead, oddly taller than
     all of them,
as if the shrinking never ends,

me drawing in the constellations they've forgotten about,

my ape arm over their soft, heart-of-zucchini shoulders,
which I would lick if they weren't already browning, noting

like a new mother who turns her face from the cemetery's
     open notebook

how, among the dippers, it's the little one
that feeds the big one.

The background noise in my part of town
comes mainly from planes that too much Dostoyevsky

and Dostoyevskyesque thinking
before bed

turns into nightmare scenarios, into shock-wave grief
flattening house after house,

all of the jet planes in flight patterns headed

from MSP to the three-letter codes that make up
this one-eye-opened sleeper's map

of a world in which the chair you've chosen to sit in
is constantly being pulled out from underneath.

Watering plants, beer in hand, in my backyard,
is like standing on the tarmac waiting for everyone.

In the telling of the story never told at all, all the calls get
    through, and all the texts,
all of the superhighways of travel
and communication

and well-wishes, as if all along they were buckets with lids

are now overfull and leaking,
are like gutted mountain ranges with their entrails spewing steamily,

so we crawl inside.

Suddenly we remember all the verses to "Amazing Grace."

Dude with a chrome nail professionally speared through the
    top of his ear
is having a blast bagging my lemonade, toothpaste, peas,

right hand shouting to left, *Incoming! Heads up!*
Somebody else will have to tell him

that when the plane you were supposed to be on, but missed,
never lands

is when you get to feel those things
that feel like wings.

I WISH I COULD TALK IN TECHNICOLOR

My brother the flamboyantly hopeful hiker goes on, doesn't turn and head for home even though I've told him, "There is no Lake Shirley"

My other brother put his father into the Salvation Army truck (the truck exhaust was a harbinger), then botched a burglary attempt at my brother who was heir to a thousand kingdoms' house. The next day's cloudy sky was the foreshadowed oracle saying, *Your addiction to giving will arrive by taxi when what you have to give, anymore, isn't anything anybody wants.* My brother the better-day-tomorrow monger cased the house of my brother who liked to fly around town with his full pelican's bill. Better-day brother tried his hand at reconnoitership disguised as a stray moose. It was in all the papers, sightings in the countryside, sightings in town. My half-moose brother didn't plan for my brother the builder of Sunday morning to be measuring and cutting cords of laziness in the adjacent backyard, a vantage that allowed him to ID the curious brother moose in a photo lineup at the DNR. "All this tranquilizing and returning to the wild!" exclaimed my two-headed brother, from his perch on the museum shelf, who despite the abundance of eyes hasn't seen a praying mantis catch and eat an unattended child yet, as my brother the sander of intentions both vague and rough, who was working in a secret embassy under the employ of the sun at the time of the latest sighting, has. My brothers my other neighbors with lives too busy to join me at this fire the light of which I'm writing this disinterested people's history by, whom I do not know, who may be burgled or cased and then will hope my builder brother isn't busy assembling a clock that will make time obsolete, and can ID the brother offender, leave their porch light on at night, all night. Why wouldn't my underpaid brothers disguised tonight as bugs throw rowdy parties there like my brothers the squatters and gutter punks do under bridges, and by the river, and in abandoned places—something my brothers fed three times daily by their handlers in their think tanks would never do. What wouldn't you think yourself capable of doing after taking the time to watch a day moth drink its fill from damp gravel? Clandestinely my brother the old poet, who they say is losing his mind, who I say is turning into a season, visits graveyards, removes the luster from polished stones. He loiters at cafes until my brothers the up-and-comers buy him breakfast. He speaks of brothers he once knew who were rich enough to buy access to power, who came to the mountain in winter to ski. He said if they had come in summer they would see the trees they mogul around growing out of rock. My brother who shares my mother said once of the body, "This machine needs some time down for maintenance." Now we all say that when we're bushed. My brother my brother watched me grill bananas marinated in brown sugar and rum, a recipe I found online. He substituted amaretto and whatnot in his own flambé. He made a better banana. He said what my other brothers need to hear when he said that the Internet doesn't know everything. So sometimes a banana is a stepping stone. And if you turn to go back, where you're going is still along a path. The last bite you had, when you held your hand out to signal I'm full, fuck if it didn't taste like wisdom.

Let's be sedentary in honor of our friends the half-buried plants

If not completely so, if we're little green chlorophyll factories,
but are unrooted, like moss, may we never be placed in a moving van,
by movers, in a move across the land.

May we never make sense of moving all the way across town.

May nothing we find important be lost.

May the only things placed in the backseats of our cars
be friends who won't fit in the front.

Let's think of the laws of time not as laws but as conventions.
We'll wear name tags and silly hats.

If we have a good enough time, we'll hit REWIND.

May the ideas we hatch and forget like dinosaur eggs
resist long droughts.

God of stuff that lasts, imbue them with the perseverance of
    alley weeds.

Make the headaches that glom like mold onto our dormant
    best intentions
wait at least until after lunch.

May we sleep and after sleep wake in a snow globe
where a tiny, mass-produced sign pointing to the right announces:
End of the Universe, 1 mile.

Because this manifesto is in part for the stomach and tongue,
may there always be peanut butter.

May the six-hundred-pound and muscular pursuit of happiness
continue to hoe and barrel cross-eyed through our china shops,
drunk on mead.

Come watch the bees with me, through this hole, making mad love
to the clover we will henceforth take our shoes off to walk through.

On behalf of the queen,
they call what they're doing work.

There is the hiding. Here is the seeking.

Nobody's here, unless you count as a somebody
an analog recording of a honey-smooth baritone voice
accompanying footage of the 1960 Olympiad
playing on a loop on a TV you get to like a lab mouse
following symbols and signs through a test maze
of haunted hallways
after a gondola ride
to the top in an empty car
that reminds you of a womb
in a lab, which makes it feel like
an experiment, this going to see
the hermit seer sage in his cave
above the tree line
on the day O Wise One goes to the village
for provisions
but leaves behind a note
in the form of a film
in which athletes are stretching
like a meadow of gentians
following the contradictory orders
of their acclaimed coaches
the breeze, the sun
over which the honey smooth voice pours out
They're in a race, and in the race
most of them will get exercise only—
only three will win a medal.
You want to protect
the ones who'll lose, like the mother
of a very large family,
a red snapper laying millions of eggs.
You want to look up the population of Las Vegas,
Shanghai, and Istanbul. You think of ten years
from one second ago, when you will feel,

if you're more than a disembodied voice,
responsible for not issuing a warning
sooner. On the way down the mountain
you understand what the seer sage
is saying: that honey-smooth will always taste
good to the tongues in our ears,
and balancing
expertly on the miniature avalanches
beneath each of your downward-angled steps
will go unheralded unless
you herald it, which isn't in your make-up,
you who now believe
your best teachers
are the ones with straight faces
telling you lies.

Lesser than

We see geese in the air. We posit takeoff,
posit landing. We see geese on the ground, in grass.
We posit a second home in water.
We would have missed the geese in the air if
not for the shadows of flying geese.
The geese we saw in grass
were wary of a dog off its leash. A bark alerted us.
We saw sentry geese eyeing the dog.
We posited nesting.
We discussed. We posit
the self as feather. We continue to posit the we
for whom the spokesperson
is me. We speak of life
as a long, long climb. Doesn't
really matter that there isn't a we here
aside from right here
where I say it. Doesn't matter that
I've been bleeding to death
for years, leaving myself on chairs
and dollar bills,
on shoestrings, in palms.
We posit getting there. We posit
a there that is nothing
like here. We breathe
heavy after an uphill stretch, hands on hips,
clasped and cupping the head. We posit
that the shadows of angels
are identical to the shadows of geese. We
whisper and we don't know why.

**If I had huge hands, and could roll the jetplane's window
down, I'd ball up the clouds and would collect them
for a future cloudball fight**

On the flip side of the Golden Gate Bridge, I note
that what this also is is a rather stunning photograph of fog's
armada amassing.

If I send a postcard to my own address, it will become a curse
I forget in a drawer

that makes me live long and suffer.

I can't fit *I ought to extract love rather than wisdom
from the next barren creek bed I come across,*

*ravishing the knuckles of stone bared and languishing there
like I'm a flash flood freeing song,*

below "Mottled coyote camouflaged on mottled hillside,"

so I write *I howl, I don't sing,
because I wasn't born with wings.*

On the back of the so-captioned *Heavy clouds competing
with sun over the Sierra Nevada,* I say that but for their passing here,

which isn't a passing in any sense of the passage of time
that you or I can wrap our tiny heads around,

mountains aren't all that, really.
A glacier I knew once told me so.

We're making a mess in the kitchen of the soon to be opened A BISTRO BY GOD, adding heretical flourishes to tater tots and grits

A telegraph signed by Anon., delivered by Paul Revere, says EX-PRESIDENTS OF THE LATTER HALF OF THE TWENTIETH CENTURY SPILLING OVER INTO THE TWENTY-FIRST ARE WORKING THE SHIFT AFTER YOU. STOP. THEY HAVE THE KEYS TO THE CLOSET. STOP. IN THE CLOSET ARE BROOMS, MAPS, RAGS, SOLVENT, GLOVES. STOP. Neither the telegraph nor Mr. Revere respect each other's work. If they didn't retreat to their respective historical corners according to the plan of god they'd fight in the kitchen of god, unfeeling toward and unaware of the ex-presidents who'll clean up the mess, fighting the way people fight in westerns, breaking chairs over each other's backs, throwing shot glasses into the big old mirror we'd like to have in our basement, in which we see ourselves practicing the sorts of smiles people will tip for. On god's behalf we're parboiling baby turtles, blanching coral for garnish, blackening the flash-frozen ribs of mammoth. This is the hell people say they'd rather be in than a heaven that resembles Des Moines. We're finally our own boss. We celebrate by laying ourselves off, awarding each other severance packages of ketchup, sugar, mustard, salt. We forget what we put in the doggy bag, do a dance you'd mistake for mating. We're glad we got full when we did. When there was a little bit left over for breakfast.

This is for you

Cool girl in stovepipe jeans
lighting a smoke at the bus stop,
your back to me,
me remembering
a morning, hot like this,
rising in the dark,
leaving early for work, going
to a job I tried not to hate
after dreaming for the first time ever
in sad-sack black
and white, up so early
I caught the grass unawares,
in the act, the lascivious
blades beneath the evergreen boughs
saying *to hell with it*, keeping on, spawning
weeds regardless of my presence.
It wasn't a storybook dawn.
It was rawer than that. More like
a caterpillar turning monarch,
cesarean-cutting
the body of a chrysalis,
birthing perfect orange, perfect green.
I bore witness to it all. I was not
the me I had hoped to be.
Before ripe turns to rot, I said, I say,
open your mouth. Swallow yourself.

Early egg cartons were made of skin and bones

I ask the double-yoked egg
if it's my grandfather's or my grandmother's soul
or both. The cardinal in the lilacs
modulating between chirp and song
is trying to answer on the egg's behalf.
I tell the grandparent egg
that what I am is an out-of-work ballad
without the money to place an ad
seeking bands. I could decoupage the egg,
hang it on a wall. In deciding to merely cook the egg,
sunny side up, in bacon grease,
put it on a piece toast
and eat it, because I'm hungry,
I'm pretty sure I know what it feels like
to be an alarm clock
that hates to herald the day.
Hard not to say *yum*
when my heart, in my grandmother's voice,
sings, *We're all shadows of one idea*
on a planet with multiple suns.
A little bit softer than that,
my brain, in my grandfather's happy tenor,
says, *Our scars aren't scars—can't you see—*
they're mouths closed like seams
waiting for the freedom to sing.
And now I know more about love.

Thinking of these awful years softly, as a lacy time preceding the water wars

The gray squirrels remind me, with their gathering
of dead stuff from the neighborhood perennials
and annuals

that winter's been spotted in their brains
that for their tiny size
splendiferously see it coming

and often after that
a task a pair of scissors or a knife does best—
        opening mail, cutting twine—
I allot to the hands or teeth

and it feels like a past life
is coaching the present one, the past life
in a car, the present one in some sort of race on foot
a stretch where the road is flat

and all morning I've been blaming things
on *The Graduate*, sure that the popularity of Dustin Hoffman
is to blame for all the poisons in our plastics

which is unfair, so I'll have to make amends
which is what the past life advises
as it hands me a beverage full of electrolytes
all dressed in jumpsuit orange

says that as a way of making things copacetic
why don't you name the smallest and most vulnerable
of the squirrels you love today
Dustin Hoffman

which I do, far enough away from spring
to have repressed the battles I lost
when I tried to stop the squirrels and their digging,
tried to save my seedlings, shoots, the daisies-to-be
I treated like words I hadn't yet said

set them in the ground, watered them
when perfection was still an option,
and a hundred miles of hope, that crazy slick road
was passable. Nobody noticed.
I knew they wouldn't, it was construction season

and so to really make AMENDS
an even longer stretch than that
is what I've started on, is why I'm here today
laying all along the east to west path of the sun
new asphalt, better even than then cool-cooked kind

a breakthrough
it sort of makes love to the old concrete
it's laid over, then convinces it
this is good

speaking with the voice of blank, blank
meaning insert the most soothing voice you know.

A cat or dog lives on the premises

You pet it as your ancestors did.
It pushes itself into the heaven of your fingers and nails.

What am I to it? is why it takes you so long
to find an unbroken bolt

with threads that match
the broken one

you're twirling like you could carve it from bone.

Globule by globule the world

Under the influence
not just of morning, or of morning just,
but of a morning after night
storms, the aftermath dripping from eaves
I thought I ought to clean
never having thought I'd witness
distillation
like this, the wild night more potent
after making its way through leaves
and gutter sludge
and at least one mourning dove's nest
doled out like eyedropper drops
like I'm a live baby thing found motherless
in grass, cradled and carried in,
and after a call to the vet
the recommendation is sustenance
a fraction of a fluid ounce at a time. Globule
by globule the world tries to coax us
from the edge
is what I come to understand
sitting beneath a tree, in dappled shade
I call Appaloosa shade
when an ant falls into my lap, then another,
god dropping ants into my water glass
because god's mischievous,
is some days even a dick,
giving the ants
life vests I can't see, but are there.
The ants never drown. They bite
my lip when I drink. I taste
blood, throw the rest of my glass
of sustenance out.
The wind, like a bulked-up body guard,

identifies the blasphemy
behind a move like that.
It wakes some more of the night's
spittle from it's slumber
on the top of leaves.
I look up. I call what's happening
raining sun. I feel like a chimpanzee
without an other, but with an un-
quenchable need to groom.

A cottonwood seed atop a blade of grass,
an I'll-never-see-anything-like-this-again-in-my-life
balancing act

Some kind of cling between them
like static attraction, like socks in the dark
that might exist only here, only now, and might owe
as much to astrology as it does to the weather,
a force that imitates what we're trying to get at
when we try to get at love
is what allows the star-seed of the cottonwood tree
to be the opposite and equal of
a blade of grass grown taller than any other
since I last mowed the yard, gave
the grasses that level playing field, that democracy,
above which the seed looks like a beacon
on top of a skyscraper, signaling
five inches from the ground,
maybe to insects.
I hold my breath so I'm not the cause
of the end of this. I have seen oh-so-many
bigger-brained others fail at connection.
This is the evidence I've been afraid I'd find
that height and achievement and genes matter,
which is sad.
I've always thought that what the mower does
is something like what the Constitution does.
All the shorter blades are watching
like this is a miracle in a movie,
dreading the credits, the breeze that ends it,
an otherwise unnoticed *shhhhhhhhh*
gentler than the sound of wind through leaves,
like applause far off, or clothes
removed in a hurry from the body,
left behind like a path of stones.

It's one thing to want one's life to be fulfilling, another to want it to be very long

A sun and a glacier sit
in folding chairs turned backwards,
the lumbar support like armor

protecting vitals in the chest. They wave
their arms as they speak. Glacier says
to Sun, "Saw a sparrow trying to crack

open the husk of a cicada on a driveway.
Never thought to use a driveway as a tool
like that." Sun says, "I know how the story

ends. The sparrow finds the husk
filled with air. Stops using tools."
Neither pays attention to the fallout

of their proximity, the melting
of one, the dousing of the other.
They take separate taxis home.

The brilliance of the sparrow
remains to be unleashed. I wake
knowing this. I eat a very small portion

of last night's supper as my breakfast.
You greet me as if it were any other
day, which it is, so you say,

Hey, how are you? I say, *Well,*
hiding the hole, the bucket, the rope,
wondering how thirsty you are.

What sort of father do you think you would have made anyway?

A flag, though less obviously patriotic as such, is more egalitarian
after it's been converted into a torch,
can spread its message writ small on tiny pieces of ash.

The people we say are stubborn as mules are harder to burn than flags.

The person we call brave is braying en route to a revolution we
    support,
else he'd be just another jackass.

What are you, if after overhearing a boy
call a more realist than impressionist elk sculpture a moose

you want there to be a test with the difference on it,
something painful the consequence for failing?

I had my hands and face slapped by my mother in public places,
am surprised I didn't grow up to be a scientist

who publishes papers people read on the toilet
that say eating dirt is good.

Go ahead: wear the skin of an animal and nothing else,
stop manicuring and bathing, strap on antlers,

perfume yourself with animal piss.

The creatures that you want to believe that you are not yourself
will still be able to tell you're not one of them.

You get to be such an old, old dog, you have to consider
what to do with the flies conferencing in and on your pelt?

It might all boil down to a foot in a shoe, and as long as it's
    petting you
a kind of complacency you call diplomacy owns the day.

To the flies in your fur you say by not saying a thing, by lying there,
If you're not the vodka or the lemonade, maybe you're the ice

that makes them a drink.

From the owner's manual

Realizing your potential is controlled by a switch on the wall.
It's a standard on/off switch.

For the price of a cheeseburger and a good beer
your handyman should be able to install a dimmer.

If, lucky you, you're handy enough to, maybe, or maybe not,
be able to install it yourself

you probably call it a *rheostat,* probably hear the word rheostat
and weep again for your dead grandfather

who left you all his money, which was none—
it's a fool who dies with it in the bank—

then took the language with the word *rheostat* in it,
the trick for installing it,

to his grave. *Realizing your potential*
being controlled as it is by a toggle on the wall,

cheeseburgers and good beers,
being in this economy semi-precious, you job-shadow handymen

like some nobody who believed it when they said
(girls) you were a princess, or that you could grow up

(boys) to be the President of the USA.

If, in rain-wet bark, you see what looks like a human face,

an officer of language law arresting the word *like*

for not living up its breeding, you'll believe,
as does the western meadowlark, anything you tell yourself.

The eastern meadowlark, which is nothing like
you or me (and is less like the western variety than you'd think)

uses the word *like* as if it were a bridge,
is always getting to the other side, flirting

with a .400 batting average.

Western meadowlarks are playing on unmarked fields.
None of them have gloves or a catcher's mitt. It's hard to be a fan.

It's a lot like life, is what Detroit Tigers Sportscaster
Ernie Harwell, and a gazillion to the tenth power others,

including the face of Jesus in the woodgrain of my bathroom door,
and men named Will Power, have said.

If they were toys there'd be dials on the meadowlarks' backs.
You could turn to the right to go from the flute-like warbling

of the western bird
to the simple whistled call of the eastern one.

Scientists say the offspring in the ranges where the sub-
        species overlap
are infertile, that it's the price of interbreeding.

What we have, then, is this break in the clouds.
Another sky where our gazes pool.

Brilliant machine that I am

What I thought was a hair in my coffee I would drink and digest,
turned out, at the true-story bottom the mug,

to be a centipede or millipede. I didn't count the legs.
I gagged a bit.

It's like getting a car and noticing a lot of other people have
    the same model,

which you didn't know existed till you had one
in your parking spot, in your driveway, your garage if you're a
    lucky cuss,

and what makes it like that is how the bug
at the bottom of my mug has made every ending since then a
    surprise,

i.e., I respond to a strange sound by turning toward it,
a slow kind of pirouette executed with both feet clumsily on
    the ground,

inventing a death dance for those who've jumped from the
    Golden Gate bridge,

like an against-the-odds flower blooming from concrete,
making a hole in it with what you thought was my flimsy stem,

which is hard to do, and I almost fall over the edge.
Lucky is you being here to grab me, me wiggling free

from an olive, from its pit,
polishing your teeth with my tiny tongue.

NORMAL

It's a planet, we've an age

On the third planet from the sun
you smoke a cigarette, or a joint,
slowly
learning patience, studying
the seat and handlebars
of a bicycle
chained to a tree
seven-eights buried
after three days of snow.
The road grader piles it on.
It's not a bully.
It's doing its job.
No matter, the bicycle drowns.
Who has the key to its lock?
It's spring
and even in spring
you wait for spring to come.

•

Welcome to the third planet from the sun.
Our disfigured cook in restaurants,
smoke on break. They talk about the night
the hot chick slow danced
with the B-teamer,
a gesture that stands
either for the end of war
or else is the seed
of all-out war
forever and ever amen. If you show up
they'll want to know which side you're on.
One of them was the B-teamer.
He says she didn't feel like a gesture.

•

If you're lucky
on the third planet from the sun, a friendly
you've never met but come to believe in
fills the candy dish, empties the trash,
tidies up while you're out to lunch.

•

Good kid says
he's digging to China. Bad kid
digs to hell. Each has a spade,
a photographic image in his head
of the other side.
Good kid taps a fork to glass,
compares the sound
to what's heard when the fork is tapped
on crystal. He eats with that fork,
calls himself *convergence*.
Bad kid taps a fork to the air,
pretends he's tapping it
on a face he loves. Both
tap the sternum with a fist, each
wants to invent a hammer made of lips
the rest of us can buy in stores
and use to see what the heart's
reflex reaction is.
On the third planet from the sun
we counsel them both to stay in school.
Once there, we tell them to study hard.

•

I do not love horses. I fear them.
I grew up in a small small town,
was a town kid, unlike Arnie Dombrowski, a farm kid

in my grade, half of a set of twins
from just outside of Mercer
which closed its school's doors
at the beginning of the great age of mergers,
the second grade to me. Arnie and his identical,
and six, eight, twelve, or fourteen others
assimilated into St. Joan's parochial.
Despite the spirit of the age of mergers,
the school didn't change its name. Around
Halloween or Thanksgiving,
during autumn I'm sure,
Arnie got kicked by a horse. He'd been feeding
animals in his father's barn, cleaning up
shit. He'd already milked the cows (a dairy age,
I'm told, preceded the great age of mergers).
The horse's shoe cut itself in miniature
in Arnie's cheek. While he convalesced on the farm
we made lists in town. Ten ways to be kind.
I wrote fifteen. Arnie returned to class
bandaged. The word I overheard
whispered nun to nun: disfigured.

·

The horse responsible for disfiguring Arnie
is the same horse I rode
in my third dream last night. Leading up
to dream number three was
dream number one: a violent thunderstorm.
I awoke to lightning and rain.
I should mention dream number two,
the recurring dream of Juanita. In it,
her hair's a horse's tail,
for Juanita was a lover of horses.
I woke with an erection
like the ones you see on fertility statues.

Dream number two was a segue
to dream number three, where Arnie's disfigurer
is a gorgeous warmblood. In the dream, I ride it
bareback, grasping its mane,
flaring my nostrils in time to its gallop.
The warmblood's haunch muscles
ripple, its swatting tail's a rudder.
The hoofs barely land. The warmblood remembers
old wings. I am, for some seconds,
the world's greatest lover of horses.

·

The meadow the warmblood and I rode in
in dream number three: chock-full of clover,
crabgrass, thistle in its purple-flower stage,
milkweeds. I wanted to break the stems off the milkweeds
to see the tiny rings of poisonous milk. Surprise
number one: the meadow wasn't endless. A strong wooden fence
made of six-by-six posts and four-by-four planks
bordered it. My mother's father leaned on a post.
He was surprise number two, in pleated gray slacks,
cuffed, black shoes. His zippered-up jacket
was the same dark gray as his slacks,
and his shirt—I could see only the collar—
was a lighter shade of gray.
It's the outfit he's wearing in the photo
taken next to the Phillip's 66 bulk-fuel delivery truck
a few weeks after his brother was killed in a wreck,
his older brother, original proprietor
of the Phillip's 66. My mother's father
did what they did back then. It was an age
either of familial piety, or of few opportunities,
or both. Grandpa climbed into the life his brother had built.
Sock, sock. Shoe, shoe. Second notch on the belt.

Wallet in the back left pocket.
Money in the front right.

·

In the photo, Grandpa is smiling and thin.
Into almost-old-age
his legs remain thin. He leaves the smile on.
His belly protrudes
like a beer drinker's does. Cancer
disables the lungs, the brain, a bit
here, a good memory there.
He loses the ability to discern
those he loves, has no appetite for food.
Every age is an age of modern medicine.
The one my grandfather died in
followed the age of bleeding out disease
via leech, and also the age of consumption,
the age of quarantine. His death
occurred at the tail end of the age whence
cancer was only ever whispered. All this happened
prior to 2050, which is more or less the time
some forward thinkers I've been reading
say we will call the dawn of the age of technology
allowing our bodies to last forever.

·

The dead in cemetery plots, and also figurines
on curio shelves, on the third planet from the sun,
can sense and predict earthquakes, pestilence,
flood, etc.. The damage to come
gets a foothold in their hollow places.
Powerless to prevent or warn, they're like wrestlers
who've lost the last match of their careers,
pulling their singlets off their shoulders,

taking a knee, not part of the spectacle,
not part of the crowd, no longer belonging
to a team. This
is a theory of mine.

•

I was stoned in a basement, drinking
Budweiser beer with the town mailman.
He had gone to school
with one of my grandpa's daughters.
He told me the daughter he was thinking of
had gotten pregnant
and was shipped away
during the age of hidden indiscretions. The mailman
said that the baby was aborted.
I learned last year, in a micro-age
in which we celebrated the airing of memoir-able laundry,
that most of what the mailman said was true. Only
he should have said *adopted*, i.e., I've a cousin
somewhere, living in the never-ending
age of blame. He or she may not know it.

•

We can't see his heart in his thumb,
thumb anxiously rubbing his trigger finger
fingerprintless, smooth. Can't see the idea of a daisy,
centuries of daisy and other petal symbology
in her pocket among the nickels, pennies, dimes.
They can't see that we can see them.
We don't know who the hell is seeing us.
Seeing is only a kind of touching, yeah,
but it's the saddest kind. Touching each other
directly with so many of us leering
would be too televised, too third planet from the sun.

One look at, and we know that touching
is the last thing we'll ever do. One look away from
says, *Man, it's the first thing we probably should.*

·

Grandpa prayed the rosary with Grandma
once a day. He promised his God he would
on the condition he return alive from Europe
after the war. I'm guessing he clutched
the beads tighter following his participation
in the age of hidden indiscretions. It was also known
as the age of daughters moving away for a year
to live with relatives in the city, or with nuns.
The tension between the him in that age
and the him in the age of the Latin Catholics
caused the cancer. Stubbing a toe can fire it up.
Ask Bob Marley. Ask his brain, lungs, liver,
and stomach.

·

Surprise number three: Grandpa, a talker,
said only one thing in the dream
in which I overcome my fear of horses.
The dream took place
during an age of not speaking
even if you are spoken to
if you know what's good for you.
Grandpa said I had disfigured Juanita,
that Juanita was not the only one. It was an age
of trying to teach opaquely
lessons you've learned firsthand.
"Opaquely," as in
"I don't know any Juanitas."

·

True story from the third planet: a warm stretch
in a cold month wakes
flies from their hidden dens
in window frames.
The character, we'll call him the man,
holds his own copy of the magazine
the character we'll call the woman
bought to read on the plane. He pronounces
the words he thinks she's reading in her head.
A fly that can barely fly
lands on his magazine.
He figures his notion of Indian summer
is what adult flies teach their larvae
to call fool's gold,
if what flies do
with their coded buzz and dance
and ramming into glass
is advise their young
based on personal experience.

·

Trusting in my sense of sound
to teach me something new, I rented and lived
in an efficiency apartment
at an intersection
where a major road crossed a minor one.
Diesel trucks were given the green light
all night, every night,
in one of the various ages
of clandestinely feeding the beast.
I wanted to learn as much as I could
so I also paid to live
in a trailer home a stone's throw from train tracks
and in miscellaneous other high-siren areas
in the age of keeping it real,

including above a bar,
where each night after closing
the patrons revved their motorcycle
engines as part of a mine is louder than yours
impromptu performance
in the age of outing our innermost selves,
and what I've found
is if you give it two weeks, the sleeping body,
for free, in the age of selling secrets,
like it's an ecosystem
ebbing, adjusts by erecting,
at each of the ears,
steel doors insulated with cork.

•

Smoke, I'm sure,
is what the moon is made of,
rising and gathering
there like we do
in the body.

This makes watching the moon
pornographic.

•

I settle on a folding chair
unfolded before a floor-to-ceiling window
in the age of Doppler weather radar, looking
for lips I can read in the clouds.
I'm just entering the age
of life lapping back upon itself,
past me's like paperbacks in a basket
in the bathroom at somebody else's place,
green clouds like an army of fears
I thought I'd defeated.

The storm's a rose.
It's not made of petals.
It's made of lips.

·

The sweaters we wear
collect hairs.

However they appear
on the head

the hairs we hold taut
are translucent

in the hand. Our skill in
decoding messages embedded in

hairs left behind
after hugs

is cold day no
feeling in the fingers

trying to read
the eroded marble

on a century-old gravestone
stuck in an age

of shivering, as if
we're inside the body of a rabbit

that the people who winter
here are trying to feed

by hand, hoping
to tame it.

·

In the age of disarmament
I saw eight birds: three grackles, three robins,
one crow, one dove. In eight bites I finished
the peanut-butter sandwich I'd fixed for lunch.
My friend Jackie answered the phone
after eight rings, arrived at my house
in his Plymouth Duster in exactly eight minutes.
He would suffer but survive, in eight months,
a fainting spell, a weak heart. Eight doctors
would plant a pacemaker
in his chest. In my bedroom, Jackie and I each had a window
to look out of, all eight contours of our noses
pressed against the screens. Mom
had turned the central air on. Jackie and I
left the windows open, allowing the thick air in. A mini-tornado
should have formed in my room. Our house sat
on high ground, some number divisible by eight
feet above sea level. My room, on the top floor,
was an eight-sided box. Across town,
a greed cloud, green wall, rolled in. Our house: soundless
till the phone rang (eight times), and mom yelled upstairs
that a tornado had scrawled its cursive
across the south side of town. No one killed.
Many houses, and the pool, and the roof
on the high school gymnasium, and the bus barn
with only seven buses inside: all gone. They said
it was a skinny tornado. Jackie and I
had been looking right where they said
it had passed. We didn't see
the skinny destroyer. My dad's dad,
on the phone with my mom, had seen it all
from his living room window, the debris
spiraling up, around, down. A neighbor's
kitchen table landed in his front lawn,
and a dead goat, and somebody's winter jacket,

and parts of walls the original owners could claim
if they recognized the markings. I saw the carnage,
lent a hand in the clean up.
That's how lucky eight's been.

•

The photos we take of each other
featuring
third planet from the sun
don't reveal how often we forget the combinations
to locks we've opened a million times. We spin the dial,
listen for a click that says spin it
the other way. As likely as not
we're stricken with arthritis
or carpal tunnel
waiting to be prepped
for an operation
a little more learning will reveal
is cosmetic. When we need it most
the last cup of coffee
pours out like tar. We put
the pen in our mouth, remember being told
never to suck on pens.

•

Like paper towels
we try to keep a little bit of everything
we touch.

•

Water-logged is what we are
when what we've waited all our lives to absorb
saunters in.

•

I'm on the metal folding chair again
in an age of incessantly threatening
wall clouds. I do not have access
to the basement, where I bet
the floor is dirt. I bet old water heaters are strewn about
like head stones in a vandalized graveyard,
purchase dates and longevity scrawled
in blue permanent marker over white
tin. The place I rent is Apartment D
during an age of landlords segmenting
the best old houses into multi-family dwellings.
D occupies portions of the second and third floors,
making one story up
as low as I can get.

•

During the age of sirens
saying seek cover
underground, I'm at the window,
ready to be mangled
and then spat out.

•

I put a foot in the stirrup, throw the other leg
around,

saddle the warmblood.
I think I can.

•

On the third planet from the sun
flight paths and highways and hallways
are the veins we flow through,
one of us always closer
to the heart.

I FEEL SORRY FOR YOU

Once a chickadee changed my life when it appeared to say without saying so, "Buddy, I represent my kind"

People thought the sun was setting.

In a mind-gram to the cognitive essence contained within a head the size of a knuckle,

turning side to side to take me in with both eyes,

I said, *The sun isn't setting, it's retreating to the hinterlands because you and I are brighter and warmer*

and have more fuel than it does.

Once can mean you will never again hold a face or breast but delicately so, that you will catch a baseball barehanded

only with unparalleled grace.

Impossible, then, to climb a ladder in that bipedal, we've come down from the trees way we usually do.

Once means you're forevermore holding the heads of ten tiny birds in the palm, ten more times two where the fingers bend,

meaning you'll circumvent instinct if you trip, you won't reach out, but will fall flat for all of us,

7 billion and counting, only your nose smashed and bloody.

That girl's skin is the parsnip I chopped for gumbo this morning white, and the way she peers into the eyes of the boy she's with, as if writ upon them are the lyrics none of the rest of us can remember, indicates she's blinded by the beauty of life

I.e., what she isn't saying is that each of us is a business, that
      our bodies are fences
around industrial parks zoned for the manufacturing of fans

that work fine for 38, 39, maybe 42 years, maybe forever,
hard to tell from fan to fan, one or two catch fire each year,

we conduct studies, move goods, make decisions based on formulas
factoring in advertising expenses, damage control,

calculating to the cent the value of a human life,
cost of a three-walled cubicle with no window view.

Those who purchase our goods are worth X to be reached.
Those who'll die from our faulty wiring receive the compensatory Y.

The last line of the story problem of our life to date,
drinking, it's clear by now, till we're drunk,

watching upstart lovers like we've caged them,
like they're our parakeets,

doesn't have to say that the value of Y must always be less than X,
that it would be smart if got something to eat,

if what we have here are entrepreneurs
who've stumbled onto something big.

We have paper left. We can make it say something else.

Only you and I would raise our hands

O moon, my moon, unabashedly, and only I would be able to
    see your hand
when the scolders ask how many of us do simple math
using our fingers.

We say, *Shorter days, have you noticed?*
when what we mean are days with a lot less light.

Same way a bawling child will either cease
when its stroller is rolled face to face with another bawling child,
or will cry in concert with the new voice,

you know exactly what I mean beyond what I'm actually saying
when I say sometimes you hope for nothing more than soft
    yolk in your eggs

and you end up with a perfect cup of coffee, too.

The best of us have bad stretches in our souls we cut out with
    butter knives.
We attach ourselves to colostomy bags full of the beautiful.

By us I mean *we two*.

Because you remind me of the solemnity/ immensity/
    veracity/ temerity
of cloudless and cold winter nights

cloudless and cold winter nights are the last vestige of a
    vengeful God
I'll make the gesture of a survival-prayer to,

my fingers crossed, speaking gibberish, pretending I'm speaking
sweet nothings to you.

In front of the TV, ironing wrinkles out, trying on my warm shirt makes me feel like cherry filling.

I've never once compared your circling to the circling of a shark, but my friend Belinda has.

Once she put her tongue in my ear.
I pretended it was yours.

When you start your car and remember you left something you need in the house, think of engaging the emergency brake not as means, but as end

Take the time to enjoy the cable tension increasing beneath your grip, a nervous system running up your back, through your shoulder, down your arm, to the wheel. Say *fuck* as shorthand for *I left what I need inside.* Now you're walk-running back to where you came from. You used to call this losing three minutes from your life. You used to eat breakfast standing up. The one you thought you left behind for the day helps you find what you need. You feel a smile like a suddenly opened flower on your face. The voice you had before it changed says, *I've been waiting to be let back in since before the Victorian age.* The one who helps you find lost things asks, *What's so funny?* You say, *I don't know. I don't know* is shorthand for *If I die right now, I don't die alone.*

BEST EVER is what I'm deeming this morning,
with its lack of disastrous news, its banana, electricity,
evidence of overnight rains

And if there's a morning after I'll greet it likewise—
Amazing grace! How sweet the sound!—announcing to it

I'm less afraid of my own old age
now than I was a month ago. A month ago

my father, a lifelong early riser with a view to the east,
across bean and corn fields, to the buildings of a town five
    miles away,

told me it took him 66 years and a missed turn in Minneapolis
to see the most liquid flame, most melting crayon sunrise of
    his life,

which was a moment for him, and he turned it into a moment for me,
same way you turn oysters and wine into a meal,

and right after he told me about the moment he said,
No wonder this city's full of deer, and me thinking I heard him
    say that

is like tapping into the mother lode of moments, and moments
being as dense as they are
my chisel against this one makes sparks

which is why your hair's on fire.

What would you make love to if the boundaries disappeared?

At the gnarly bases of fences, where mowing machines can't reach,
this due to the housing of the blades, the protecting of the feet,

is where our inclination for self-preservation meets our
    engineering abilities,
and byproducts happen, in this case a subtle kind of lawlessness,

grass growing taller than it ought to, weaving, or not,
through the chain link,

cueing in anti-disambiguous, never prized as a pet,
sometimes omnivorous me

all the lessons I'm still learning from, spoken and un,

a teacher in a wheelchair who wanted me to reach
but not just *reach* or *reach out. Reach*, she said, *across through
inside beyond amid.*

She would've hated the fence, made love to the grass.

The byproduct of imagining that your teacher is a high dark wave
rolling out of her wheelchair, getting it on with fescue,

is taking 40th to Lyndale in such a state of limitlessness
that the one of me walking feels like two of me,

like the spirit dragging the carcass across the ocean floor,

which is one way of reaching nontraditionally, but what my teacher

who is by now asleep in the grass
and is fair game for attack by the cocooning morning glories

meant by *really reaching* is that my next step is a stepping
out from nestling, from the over and undergrowth, the ferns
    and bramble,

71

my good-student heart a cardinal redder than red, outside of theory, should ever be allowed to be.

The finger pads may callous because of it

and you'll have to be wary of the lack of discipline
inherent in the high-strung thumbs,

but once during your time in the body
convince another

to shut down access
from all the side roads,

touch like you'll scare the touched away,
will change the touched irrevocably,

as if the touched crumble
beneath the weight of opening up
to touch,

like you were touching yourself
who upon being touched

by yourself
would no longer be
yourself,

a touching without thinking
of being
inside of,

like you're a presidential motorcade
passing through.

Because I'm made up of soldiers from opposite sides celebrating, together, the end

I'm going to chew off a shitty part of my life,
follow a black-magic recipe requiring tails of newts,
     fingernails of virgins,
the boiling of, drinking of, and bathing in it,

so that, as with the keenest lizards,
something new will grow in shitty's place.

If your car stops running, I'll chew on it.
Let me know if your cat is sick.

Call a plumber if your toilet's broke.

Call me if you feel like DNA extracted from the whole,

like you're being tested in a lab
to see if you match what you are no longer a part of.

Because I added the reproductive glands from four species of oyster
collected by widows in four different seas

I can apply my spittle to the missing and lost
to summon both healing and return.

Call me if you lost your leg in war. If your daughter ran away.
If your keys are shaking yet you're in no hurry to leave.

The consensus opinion on the evals is your faith in my mouth
won't hurt much.

Call if you gave yourself to another like a message in a bottle
that broke or sunk or got eaten by a shark.

If you've forgotten the words to a song you'd like to sing
to an empty chair.

That tree there (from the perspective of this poet here) doesn't have to fall to be heard

The uneven contractions in its trunk, knobby and bulbous growths,
like a sculpture of the unfair distribution of wealth,

or of the chasm between that which can and cannot
grow in the throes of shade,

a perpetual yearning inherent in the limb reaching down,
as if it should have been born a root and will henceforth be
    remembered

as a very bad year that seemed, when it began, like a good one,

trying to make sense of it, cramming each regularity and quirk
into periods, eras, schools, styles, movements,
naming them for people I know who are like that,

I'm stunting the tree's growth, imprisoning it like a digital
    camera can.

In less than two minutes I've screwed myself up,
rationalizing (and re-rationalizing) the needles at the tip,

trying to come up with (to admit to) something other than
    faithfully seeking.

The variegated bark represents the various responses of wood
to draught or flood, that's all, I convince myself,

so that I might stop seeing the tree as a mirror reflecting me.
The tree's coniferous, a dropper of cones.

I pick up the ones that are pocket-sized.

I bet they'll make good kindling.

Ode to sumac[1]

What fills my head planting sumac, proprietor of my own happiness,
happiness an abstraction closely related to sumac,

is a picture of roots like cast out nets under everything I step on.

Hard to tell if the earth tolerates or embraces my work.

I ask earth's concubine, the air, carrier of pathogens, of plague,
air that at night takes on the black of earth,

if what I'm doing is done at angels' or demons' behest.

The air says nothing, as if to say *go on*.

I dig into soil like a tick after blood.
Showing you mine is what I'm doing

so that you'll be coaxed into showing me yours.
Digging so that I'll be dug into.

Will be infiltrated by one that wants to live by leaving itself
untraceably inside of another.

Dirt stains like bad milk at the corners of my mouth.

---

1   Because if you can't beat it, join it, i.e., it's impossible to stop it from
    spreading—mowing the shoots gives you two or three sumac-free
    days, tops—and, fyi, were this an ode not only to sumac but also to
    making out, what you'd overhear me say is, "Lips as red as sumac
    leaves in fall," then, "Thank you, ma'am, may I have another."

**You are mistaken if you think I am speaking
figuratively or am lying when I say I speak
better wood duck than I do Latin or Greek**

Most days it feels like a not too sweet
not too tart fruit is fermenting
between my ears, which I can never have a taste of,
my brain like one of those books
they won't let people like me check out,
only experts get to see what it says there
with gloves and a mask on
under supervision
in a climate-controlled room.
The rest of us get a summary.
Doing what experts do
must be like coming to the being-built
horizon, where the rebar's just begun
to pierce the void, where the secret within the secret
within resides. I'd like to swim
in the heads of the people who say the things
the rest of us repeat to death
and also in the heads of animals who intuit
things I don't, and by swim I mean like a non-swimmer
without a life vest on, like a virus
that makes its way in through the mouth
or nose or skin. Best part of the week
is when it feels like all five-foot-ten of me's
glowing from toes to lips, the way a cat's ear does
when the sun shines through it,
which happens to me only when I give
me the afternoon off, which is what I was trying to say
when I said I spent the time
right up to lunch not thinking about the $5 taco bar
but in an imaginary conversation with Tom
who said, during our "Reveal a Secret to a Stranger"

icebreaker, that he was the only Lutheran
in Minnesota who didn't have a taste
for hot dish. What I wanted to ask him,
but didn't—a speaker from an organization
that had won awards was taking the stage—
is did he mean the hot dish with tater tots,
or the kind with rice, or my favorite
with the potato-chip crust
made with a can of cream of mushroom soup
as its base, as if without knowing that
I wouldn't know what he meant at all,
making what we'd done there, in that room,
a waste of our time together.

May we bask, like mussels, in white wine and garlic, costing what we're worth once you factor in our capacity to be loved

May we stay on the menu for a very long time.
May *cliché* have the same connotation as *emeritus*.

We'll say it and say it and say it, everybody will say it's true.
Everybody will be on the guest list.

Landlords will leave the party singing, *May the thermostat in my house control the temperature in all of my rental units.*

When your faucets drip, may mine.
May your cold, cold showers runneth down my back.

We'll write books based on the lessons of the Floridians
who turned *cockroach* into *palmetto bug*.

We'll become a delicacy smothered in chocolate.

Extremophilic life will be discovered on one of the newest of new
planets before we die. You'll have to listen closely.

Priests from then on will lowercase the G
when they say *god*.

We'll try very very hard to convince the city lights to free their
    hostages
the Milky Way and stars. We'll be a delegation of one.

We'll make a comeback as a small plate, an appetizer.

We'll be like abandoned swimming pools in forgotten
    Olympic villages.
Weeds growing through our cracked concrete will love our
    emptiness.

People are watching.
We'd be embarrassed if we knew this.

I missed your wake but hope to make your funeral

Come tomorrow, today will be like a mattress
flipped, the side I'm sleeping in now
        turned down,

                the ethery aftermath
                of my travails

                        poured out.

Today, the car stalls. The rain turns
to freezing rain.

                I accept the gift of buoyancy
                offered by the community of stones

                        that make up the gravel shoulder
                        of the road.

What I know I know

        not like an actuary does,
        but like a mole:

how the hood's release latch fits
between vulnerable fingers,

                        the difference between finger work
                        and fingering,

                that fingertips
                are natural-born scouts.

I have gone in clean,
come out specked in black.

I know the pressure it takes
to achieve slide. I have practiced with mirrors,
with mouthing

> how to share bad news
>> in the eyes-down way
>> the oncologists I've met
>> do it.

> I know fingering
> primeval, how it feels when my hands
> become machine.

I lean into engine trouble
> like bird feeding bird

in anticipation of a message
> from an isolated sense

> I think of
> as a tiny mechanic.

>> I let him crawl from my mouth.
He reads the engine's Braille, wields tools
like a dancer working castanets.

>> The community of stones
>> looks up in unison

>> as I am looking down

making the angels on high
version of dying

quaint. I jump in place,
> jostle and warm
> the blood. Hearing

nothing, I'm reminded of the empty promise
of the timpani drum.

No one chooses to be a wire brush.
No one chooses to be a snare skin.

I button a button
I never thought the wind would ask me to use.

The bad news is this: It's a long walk.
I'll be late and soaked and filthy
and will have to change into somebody
else's clothes.

No decree I know of
prevents rock and blacktop
from marrying.

I kick stone onto road,
stone onto road,
stone onto road.

Every view is oceanic if you focus on the sky

There will be other times,
like now, when it's important I not make a sound,
when it helps to think of myself
as cup to the brim full of hot stuff
traversing the top support pole on a chain link fence,
acrobatically balancing
so as not to spill anything
out of my head. Boxers who bob and weave
have a hard time doing this.
Given the inherent unfairness of life, the boxer
I want to be is the one who makes it
through the fifteenth round, demands a rematch
before the judges have said who's won.
Whether I plant my chair
in shade or sun, I'll open up
like the flower the chair has made, clipping my nails,
gathering the slivered moons of me,
blowing them from my palm
isn't mockery, it's an offering, and the best
advice I have for the harvest moon
I'm offering my nails to
is even if the jellyfish is dead, it can sting, and if it stings
somebody'll have to piss on your feet.
Some jellyfishes, before the tide
or storm beaches them, have committed
a map of the stars to memory.
I hear machines building a bridge.
I heard nothing when the green fields and grass
were painted gold.

**The sky's agenda has no Google, Microsoft, you,
me, Supreme Court, China, or offshore wind turbines on it**

I'm waiting for leaflets to litter my yard,
to be carpet-bombed and bunker busted, as if the heart
I harbor were an enemy thing. I tell the sky
that for nine years I listened to a daughter
with a one-item agenda.
I heard a mother relent. Nine
generations of mayflies
is how a middle-aged walleye
counts that. The puppy learns to come
to Patches. Kind of dog I'd love best
wouldn't do a thing for you
if you called it
the same name twice.
I'd love to know if an egg
is as great a thing to live inside of
as it seems to be. This point of view's
the point of view of the hatched
in a mean mean world. Once
I was forever changed by a brush
not with death, but with a willingness to give up
life for a cause. I don't remember
what the cause was. Never wrote it down.
Has everything to do with
why sitting, the day an unfilled-in blank,
feels sometimes like running
on a stress-fractured ankle, other times
like labored flying, like I'm trying to do it
with surgically adhered wings.

You should take the wheel

What I learned riding in the back and passenger seats as a kid
is that the people who gave me shelter and food

and things for my birthday

responded to amber lights by hitting the gas. I hit the gas.
A sky that's used-water gray on a background of black

laced with green
is saying expect violence from above.

I back off the gas.
The ambulance we all pull over for,

which feels like being chivalrous, like holding open a door,
after it passes us half a block up

shuts its lights and siren off,
turns the corner

slowly, waits in line behind two other cars—
one's a Honda—at a red light.

One thing you can do when death passes you by
is order barbequed chicken, or an enchilada, or get your hair done,

or the materials you need for your August projects

if you're at the corner of 38th and Nicollet
where you can get those things pretty cheap.

What I'm doing is pretending I'm a kid who's lost hold
of his helium-filled balloon,

that my frog's tongue of arm
can grab it back.

Shadows late in the afternoon speak with a southern accent

Dialect of the tree as it grows out of last year's shoes,
performs its silent musical based on the life of John Keats.

The sun speaks a dying language,
consequence of willy-nilly taking the life of border crossers

ditched or lost in deserts.

It's like the simmering of a crowd
which will disperse before it asserts
its will.

Try being happily married to the incomprehensible,
sharing coffee with it several times a day.

One day I'll dress in shiny leather, will open the invitation,
plot a fashionably late arrival.

None of what happens afterward would've happened
if the kiss hadn't been so good.

Sad that the taste doesn't last.

I kiss the ground and flowers, walls and fur, my tongue like a brook
going low spot to low spot,

over rocks, bringing and depositing sediment,

which builds up, provides desirable land for growing,
for building domiciles on.

O green and white porcelain, O representation of frog

Two black slits for a nose. Black slits for claws. Forelegs
splayed, holding together a fissure at the bottom

of the flower pot I found you in, in a window box,
in a house I'm sprucing up.

Some maker decided your ears ought be a shade of yellow
with more white mixed in than the mustard color

used for your eyes. I'm moving you to the grass.
Good thing you weren't left in a well

I couldn't reach to the bottom of.
I'm hungry for seafood, for frog legs.

The someone who left you behind
is from a long chain of someones, only one of whom

once glued your leg back on.
The repair seam circumnavigating your shoulder

wasn't part of the plan of the maker who forgot to
or cruelly didn't give you a mouth.

If I carry you everywhere I go, it will be like learning
rudimentarily how to parent.

If you were a TV that didn't work, and I left you on the curb,
somebody would have eviscerated you by now

for all the copper and whatnot within.
Latent inside you, is that the urge to burrow?

Don't let me stop you from turning into a toad.
It would be cruel to leave you outside for even one more
    beautiful night.

Something along the lines of flirting practice
is a person imagining himself kissing a cracked glass thing

in case it shape-shifts.

Something along the lines of embarrassment practice has that
    person asking,
What would I do with a prince?

If I happen upon paint and a brush, I'll have to decide if life
is better with or without a mouth.

Let me get out of this shirt.
We'll dance and sing our praises to Elmer's, Krazy,

all manner of glue. What I'm saying is I want to call you
STALLED IN THE MIDDLE OF THE ROAD.

You call me PUSHING THE TRUCK WITH ALL EIGHT ARMS.

Of how we'll cope with our roles in the scheme of things,
you have your baked-on crust of glaze

and I'm going to put my shirt back on.
I'm not going to kiss you. Neither am I going to throw you

against a wall. I won't strap razors to your legs,
toss you into a ring, or drop you into the trash

that the garbage truck picks up tomorrow.

Maybe tonight I'll clear some space, set you on my pillow.
Maybe I'll call it a lily pad.

The ribs and sternum being no kind of fence

I'm going to take my jacket off, let my heart see the leaping fishes
and standing bears that emerge from a tree trunk

once a chainsaw's taken to it.

Pepper-shaped, my heart itches like a wound
just sealed, just beginning to heal.

Having exposed it, I suppose the sun will purple it
so it never blends in.

Why not use a gnat as the thing that best describes
my ability to keep my heart in my chest, off my sleeve,

as in, *I have the self-control of a gnat.*

A spider my size could carry a house on its shoulders
if it had them,

but gnats and spiders and hearts only grow to be our size in movies
with bloody beginnings, middles, ends.

My heart was a hand. It became a fist.
The story I like to tell

is it closed around a star.

Notes

Thank you sincerely to the editors of the journals who first published poems from this book, and to Amy Berkowitz who made a handful of them into a chapbook;

to the Minnesota State Arts Board for a grant that allowed me to read these poems, and to work through them and the book, at venues across the country, and to venue hosts Chris Tonelli, Jen Woods, Dustin Luke Nelson, MC Hyland, Jeff Peterson, Debrah Morkun, Anne-Adel Wight, Aaron Tillman, Matthew Lippman, Adam Fell, and Ryan Collins;

to Lisa Sisler for her editorial direction and vision, and to all of the editors and staff at Trio House who selected this book;

to the kind and amazing Lee Ann Roripaugh, Aimee Nezhukumatahil, and Bob Hicok;

to the brother-sister poets and poetry fanatics that comprise the scene in Minneapolis and St. Paul, which has more-than-earned the moniker "Poetry City, USA";

to Paula Cisewski, Matt Ryan, Dobby Gibson, and Matt Rasmussen, poet-friends who continue to help me find my way as a poet;

to Steve Healey, who fits into the aforementioned category, but who also provided detailed and astute analysis of this book, and made me a different and better writer;

to my immediate and extended family for their unflagging support;

to my number-one fans Wednesday and Zooey, to you for buying this book, and to anyone I've missed whom I shouldn't have;

and to Angie, who makes it all matter.

Matt Mauch is a fiscal year 2012 recipient of an Artist Initiative Grant from the Minnesota State Arts Board. This activity is made possible in part by a grant from the Minnesota State Arts Board, through an appropriation by the Minnesota State Legislature and by a grant from the National Endowment for the Arts.

MINNESOTA
STATE ARTS BOARD

Acknowledgements

Versions of the following poems have appeared in the following journals, sometimes with a different title:

Salt Hill: "The sky's agenda has no Google, Microsoft, you, me, Supreme Court, China, or offshore wind turbines on it," REPRINTED on *Verse Daily*;

H_NGM_N: "There is the hiding, here is the seeking"

NOÖ Journal: "Because I'm made up of soldiers from opposite sides celebrating, together, the end"

Squaw Valley Review: "Lesser than"

Paper Darts: "A cat or dog lives on the premises"

The Adroit Journal: "BEST EVER is what I'm deeming this morning, with its lack of disastrous news, its banana, electricity, evidence of overnight rains," "What would you make love to if the boundaries disappeared?," "Ode to sumac"

Connotation Press: "What sort of father do you think you would have made anyway?," "If, in rain-wet bark, you see what looks like a human face"

LEVELER: "That that girl's skin is the parsnip I chopped for gumbo this morning white, and the way she peers into the eye of the boy she's, as if writ upon them are the lyrics none of the rest of us can remember indicates she's blinded by the beauty of life"

InDigest: "Thinking of these awful years softly, as a lacy time preceding the water wars," "To survive is to lament, so let's all do it well"

Blood Lotus: "When you start your car and remember you left something you need in the house, think of engaging the emergency brake not as means, but as end"

Water~Stone Review: "It's a planet, we've an age (fragment 11)"

South Dakota Review: "Every view us oceanic if you focus on the sky," "A cottonwood seed, a blade of grass, an I'll-never-see-anything-like-this-again-in-my-life balancing act"

Midway Journal: "It's a planet, we've an age (fragment 15)"

Spinning Jenny: "If had huge hands, and could roll the jetplane's window down, I'd ball up the clouds and would collect them for a future cloudball fight"

ILK: "Only you and I would raise our hands," "Shadows late in the afternoon speak with a southern accent"

Toad: "From the owner's manual"

The Chariton Review: "My brother the flamboyantly hopeful hiker goes on, doesn't turn and head for home even though I've told him, 'There is no Lake Shirley,'" "The ribs and sternum being no kind of fence," "O green and white porcelain, O representation of frog"

Revolver: "Early egg cartons were made of skin and bones," "Globule by globule the world," "That tree there (from the perspective of this poet here) doesn't have to fall to be heard"

Strange Machine: "May we bask, like mussels, in white wine and garlic, costing what we're worth once you factor in our capacity to be loved"

Fragments 19, 21, 22, 23, 24 and 25 of "It's a planet, we've age," under the titles "It's a planet, we've an age (a fragment)," "It's a planet, we've an age (another fragment)," "It's a planet, we've an age (further fragmentation)," and "It's a planet, we've an age (a fragment in flagrante delicto)," plus "It's one thing to want one's life to be fulfilling, another to want it to be very long" appear in the chapbook *The Brilliance of the Sparrow* (Mondo Bummer)

About the Author

Matt Mauch is the author of *Prayer Book* (Lowbrow Press) and the chapbook *The Brilliance of the Sparrow* (Mondo Bummer). He hosts the annual Great Twin Cities Poetry Read, and also the Maeve's Sessions readings, and edits the anthology *Poetry City, USA*, an annual collection of poetry and prose on poetry. A 2011 recipient of a Minnesota State Arts Board Artist Initiative Grant, his poems have appeared in numerous journals, including *Salt Hill, H_NGM_N, DIAGRAM, Willow Springs, The Los Angeles Review, South Dakota Review, Sonora Review, Water~Stone Review, ILK, NOÖ Journal, InDigest,* and *Spinning Jenny,* and on the *Poetry Daily* and *Verse Daily* websites. Mauch teaches creative writing at Normandale Community College, and lives in Minneapolis.

About the Book

If You're Lucky Is a Theory of Mine was designed at Trio House Press through the collaboration of:

Lisa Sisler, Lead Editor
Annie Stoll, Graphic Design
Dorinda Wegener, Cover Design
Lea C. Deschenes, Interior Design

The text is set in Adobe Caslon Pro.

The publication of this book is made possible, whole or in part, by the generous support of the following individuals and/or agencies:

Anonymous

About the Press

Trio House Press is a collective press. Individuals within our organization come together and are motivated by the primary shared goal of publishing distinct American voices in poetry. All THP published poets must agree to serve as Collective Members of the **Trio House Press** for twenty-four months after publication in order to assist with the press and bringing more Trio books into print. Award winners and published poets must serve on one of four committees: Production and Design, Distribution and Sales, Educational Development, or Fundraising and Marketing. Our Collective Members reside in cities from New York to San Francisco.

Trio House Press adheres to and supports all ethical standards and guidelines outlined by the CLMP.